THREE-WAY STREET

Published by Koo Press — 2004

Sheila.13@btinternet.com

Typeset in 12 point Garamond

ISBN 0-9542076-3-7

Contents

Gerard Rochford

Eddie Gibbons

Douglas W Gray

Gerard Rochford

TROTH

Blackbirds stay together, close down their choices,
work, keep faithful, and when the female sits
the male rejoices
into and out of the darkness.

So sometimes I think
why can't we just get along?
Is love, even when damaged,
so unusable? Isn't the mend more strong?

What eludes us
is the tending and letting it lie
in a settled garden,
within warm walls, beneath the acoustic sky.

In lives as ordinary as loaves,
with a hunger for more than we have known,
we hope that being grown up
is just putting on grown-up clothes.

Nothing prepares us, not even vows,
for this ragged nest
and the shock of children
with their open mouths.

Yet blackbirds perform their duty
to the end of time;
they keep in line,
and hold a tune of beauty.

ESSENCE

for Rosie age 8

Where is God? God is everywhere
(Catholic catechism)

Suddenly you stopped
to feel a leaf.

It was Christmas,
cold, but you stopped;
a casual sacrament,
communion in the hand.

As we stood, our streetlight
flickered and went out.
You looked up, frowned,
still holding to the leaf.

Such unity of soul,
of leaf, of hand,
reaches to the moment
of Creation;

stalling the infinity
of now, of leaf,
of you,
within the keeping of the night.

And then we journeyed home,
like Magi from a birth.

THE ISLANDER — AGE NINE

Fintan draws boats,
always boats,
boat after boat after boat.

He breathes life
into the blank sails,
zephyr of his mind's map.

With clenched fist
he scribbles black looks
into the yawning stacks.

Today he is drawing another;
scowling he journeys
to the cutting edge.

Now he's back home,
a steady floor,
mother, the smell of food.

He sleeps at anchor,
dreaming the swell of love and anger,
rising falling leaving returning.

He is in harbour,
till another moon
pulls at the tide of his searching.

THE FROG PRINCE

for Xander age 10

Through the front door you run
and out the back
with hardly a greeting.

You are dashing to see your frog,
which lingers with intent
in its damp estate.

Sometimes the marshy hunchback
is at home; a watchful green purse,
a cool wee bellows.

Sometimes it's away.
You search with torch,
with beating heart, with dread.

You are learning love and loss,
the emptiness of hands,
the dappled beam of hope.

You live between a scuffed sky
and the earth with its web of roots.
You are a prince of unkent purposes.

TIC-TOC

...so then I said:
do you two have children?

He broke in:
no way!

And though her face showed hurt
was it her womb that wept?

The felt skin of a rose
turns fissile and dull when cut;

gathered into the home
some depth of red remains.

Bloody seasons
pulse her veins;

thrawn memos
to her cursed desire.

HAIKU LOVE STORY

Chapter 1

she says I love you
a clean moon is stained with cloud
he cannot say it

he wants to fuck her
so he whispers I love you
they're both taken in

orange blossom falls
tells him the news from within
still no wedding day

Chapter 2

you never loved me
you knew that when we married
kid scared— mind abused

mum where's my dad gone?
don't know son and don't much care
fags— chip pan— fire risk

Chapter 3

dad's quality time
child support— what a laugh
thank God for thrift shops

your dad's got a job
he can't take you out this month
like I believe him

saw him in The Green
he's got another woman
both pissed— she's pregnant

what's a half-brother?
dads have two lives— mums have half
you have not a lot

Chapter 4

what does dad look like?
like you son— your eyes your nose
that right? well fuck him

GRALLOCH

The act of disembowelling a deer
killed in a hunt

(i)

You may experience
slight discomfort;
there might be
some seepage.

I won't need
to see you again,
unless there's pain
or excessive bleeding.

(ii)

Upon my sterile bed,
beneath the scan
of brash lights,
I hear a screaming.

I will keep
those barren birthdays;
remember the boy
who promised love.

PUTTING IT RIGHT

for Ishbel

She cuddles her children,
no memories to sustain her;

keeps them clean,
where she was clothed in shame;
skims off guilt,
where she was got heavy with sin.

She is their amulet,
she shines;
while deep within
she craves
the unreachable hand of love.

She has felt
through the bars of a cold cot
the frosted pane of dawn;
the moon holding on,
the sun grasping the day.

She is making her claim
beyond the glen of revenge;
deeply divining
the river line of her life.

Slowly she builds her fire,
breathes on the ash of her past.

VOYEUR

I watch
at my window.

She is feeding her young:
me! me! me!

At every coming
they stretch priapic;

penis-necked
and gagging.

These stiffs
are alive and well;

treble their size
in a week;

mimic
all that counts.

BLACKBIRDS

Son, two months old
and bigger than mother.
She calls the tune,
lets him feed— or not.

Stark yellow his beak
this oedipal coward;
and mum's a freak
with a whitey neck.

Dad's a rock star.
Black for real, jet;
ace near spades
for worms.

She's worn thin
but tough as nuts;
cracks a snail at dawn.
He's gigging up a tree.

Does she mind the Spring
of fertilise and song?
Next year
will hatch again.

THE SHADOW OF A QUESTION

for Lisa

Could you forgive me
if I was unfaithful?

I could
but I wouldn't,
she says,
turning away.

He feels the ice
of her asunder;
knows a pain
he has not suffered—
dared to cast before her.

The ring that binds him
is placed
in her strong hold;

where love,
rare as a fallen angel,
can be sharp
with fear.

But bright, bright.

THREE

When through the heavy earth of sleep

she raised her lover's name

he knew

from the rut in her voice

he shared the occupation of her bed

but all the slow bleeding

was his

and his alone.

MISCARRIAGE

The only one
she could not bear
was planted
like a cutting;
covered its story
in red earth.

He knew the exact spot,
waited for nothing
to strike;
while in his dreams
that tiny hand
tightened around his heart.

HEALING

She left with scant clothes,
the dog unfed,
a pencilled note.

"I have gone— I am sorry."
He read it over and over;
it did not change from grey.

Ash in the grate grew damp;
dust gathered,
even on webs.

Raspberries rotted;
a stupid thrush still sang
when the sun cleared off.

Then, Autumn registered.
He picked an apple,
relished its juice.

EVENING SHORELINES

A starfish lies dead,
riddance from the sea;
outreached itself
on the hackled wave.

I flip it over;
sand spoils the mouth,
soils the cerecloth skin.

I gouge a grave
with my heel,
scuff its pallor
into the seeping hole.

This cover-up
has robbed a child
of that grim lesson.

The sky switches on
like an alien city;
the ocean bed
a galaxy of birth.

ELEMENT

Icarus the lark
and the wren Orpheus
sing, each in their own dominion.

As we do;
revealed by the style of our rejoicing
and our conspicuous silences.

Alert amid the slough and scabs of earth
or rising through the sun's kingdom of gold,
we search for nutrients and burnished gods;

until the landscape fades,
all detail lost
that gloried in the late slanting light.

EATING EGGS WITH STRANGERS
NEAR BUCKFAST ABBEY

for Peter and Mimi

The brother of my friend
greets me;
his wife beautiful
as an actress.

They are laughing.
In garden warmth
we drink red wine
for the soft easing of blood.

Suddenly, he fancies
cold boiled eggs
with salt;
communion white,

thigh smooth,
modest erotica,
in the afternoon
of their summer.

No cloud,
no breeze,
no chanting
from the monks.

These pure forms
are grace enough,
meeting this man,
this woman.

MEETING MRS MCKENZIE AND HER HUSBAND

Foolishly I said:
are you still singing?

She gave me a look;
he smiled. Then I remembered:

it wasn't her who sang
those faded years ago.

And yet, was I right
to sense a gift unwrapped,

bound with wire,
rusted by tears,

snagging
their close-knit love?

THE DINING TABLE

So many times we sat here,
book ends,
holding the stories of our children.

It rests on legs of beech;
deep drawers are crammed
with nostalgic paraphernalia:

a '25' silvered for a cake,
childrens' paintings,
negatives, a French coin.

This table holds more secrets than a bed;
unspoken words shiver like knives,
peacemakers smooth as spoons.

Come time
one of its legs will falter,
a forest of memory felled...

For friends I spread a damask cloth,
which settles
like the open wings of a moth.

Red wine will bleed on bread
and white wine glasses weep,
in the warmth of a chill night closing.

NOSTALGIA

for Michael Dennis Browne

There is no road back.
Travellers know this
as their stubborn boots
beat the ungiving ground.

Tangled memories
catch at our days like bramble
and lost lovers
crowd around our dreams.

Wounds and wants unbalance our mind
with attics and basements of slag,
shifting the weight of our heart
away from its centre.

We may climb the heaven-bent tree
our father planted
and we may honour
its searching roots;

but the home is here.
Fling out the tattered banners of the past
and fly the bright flags of now
with their startling colours.

SEPARATIONS I

Through beams of dust the newsreel scours the past.

Soldiers culled from slums,
fags in smiles of rotting teeth,
march with song
to bleed and drown in mud;

evacuees with gas masks,
corralled by mothers,
are labelled and counted
onto smoking trains;

death-camp travellers,
branded into trucks,
clutch all they own,
swaddled, in their arms.

They wave a flag of bone from frozen lives.

SEPARATIONS II

My memories were sepia clad then framed in super-eight.

Fixed in doorways,
platforms, barriers,
they flicker and fade
down corridors of loss.

My father, crying,
waves to my brother;
the father
whose hand I shook,

repeats his father's rite,
away to school as child,
to war while still a boy,
fearing the single journey.

My children
now migrate.
I call out:
see you later.

Auf Wiedersehen. My hand flares like a bird.

Eddie Gibbons

DRINKING PARTNER

You're sitting alone, drinking.
Could be espresso,
could be cappuccino,
could be a cup of cold tears.

To avoid the eyes
of huddled couples
you place a sheet
of paper on the table.

A poem sidles up to you
and drinks your pen dry.

CHIAROSCURO

She is sleeping still
in the wide-awake world.
She is distant as Charon
though she sits at his shoulder.

Her words are mists rising
from an iron ground.
Tears well from the eyes
of the woman drowned within.

Her every action is the shielding
of a shuttered sadness.
She is veiled in the window
of a room hoarding shadows.

Soon he will enter her like daylight.

FLARE

I see it this way:
you heated, flared, boiled over.
I tried to dampen, douse, cool,
but simply fuelled.

You erupted like Krakatoa.
I was ice floe, hoar frost,
glacier; pure refrigeration.
You were Fahrenheit, I was Kelvin.

You were molten throughout
the palaver; hot as a solar corona.
I was cat-calm, composed, serene
while you vented your spleen.

You fumed, flamed, blazed,
like you'd swallowed hot lead.
Come on — spit it out —
was it something I said?

VARIATION ON A DREAM DEFERRED

Good morning, daddy!
Who's that bird?

Darling, she's my
dream deferred—
my final chance,
please take my word.

Daddy, we will hate you now
you're leaving us for that cow!

Good morning, mummy!
Ain't you heard?
Daddy's gone and got affaired!

FORFEIT

You forfeited your life the night you left
the sleeping family who you could not face.
And now: the triumph of a suitcase
at your feet as you try to thumb a lift.
Then headlights turn your way, the evening's gift
is a Vauxhall Astra heading for the coast.
You talk but see the driver isn't fussed,
so you're counting all the hurts that caused the rift.

You're counting all the hurts that caused the rift:
the brief affairs, the drudge, the way she fussed;
the joyless holidays on some grim coast,
the children, matrimony's only gift.
Then suddenly a screech, you feel the lift
of the impact crumpling your suitcase
and shattered glass embedding in your face.
You forfeited your life the night you left.

HAD I BUT KNOWN

Had I but known
that kiss would be the last kiss,
that caress the final touch,
I would rather have died
where I stood—
your breath on my face,
the taste of you still on my lips,
my heart as yet unwithered.

MEMO TO MYSELF

There are days when simply
being here is not enough:
days when you stop
your aimless dithering
and trace your footsteps
back to the early world
you used to live in.

This is the source
of your happiness
and anger. This is the glow
that keeps you warm,
the fire in which you'll burn.

And when you've cast aside
all the luggage of your burdens
and catalogued the items
in your universe,
you will be left alone
with your unquenched desires
and the full and final knowledge
that this is the hell
everyone
has always warned you of.

SHORT MEASURE

When you left me,
you left me this—
a lovelorn duvet
bereft of bliss,
a one-hit wonder
short of a Miss,
a trouser snake
that's lost its hiss,
and two lips
short of a kiss,
a kiss,
two lips short
of a kiss.

DESIRED ERRATA

Dear Miss X,
There were several typographical errors in your recent
love letter to me. I return it to you for the necessary
amendments.

For *we* read *me*
For *is* read *was*
For *you* read *who?*
For *love* read *shove*
For *cherish* read *perish*
For *wanton* read *wanting*
For *undying* read *denying*
For *breathless* read *lifeless*
For *sweetheart* read *weepheart*
For *infatuation* read *trepidation*
For *engagement* read *estrangement*
For *monogamy* read *monotony*
For *foreplay* read *beforeplay*
For *laughter* read *slaughter*
For *darling* read *snarling*
For *panting* read *parting*
For *Eros* read *errors*
For *tongue* read *tied*
For *ring* read *sting*
For *you* read *her*
For *sex* read *ex*

Yours Unfaithfully,
Mr. Y

KIDDO

In answer to Simon Armitage's 'Kid'

Robin, small fry, when I gave the warder
the thumbs up, then let you loose to squander
the leeway, did you not stop to ponder
what I had to say? Or blanked me, rather
with a mutter... well, I give the orders.
Now you've botched that 'he was like a jailer
to me' rumour, sucker, undercover
of that 'he was like a nagging mother'
story, dished the dirt to all the papers
on Lois Lane and me, how I took her
to the phone booth, foiled that Clark Kent caper.
Holy Batman-Lois-phone-romp-shocker!
Holy comic-hero-gets-leg-over!
I'm not seeing Batgirl any longer
Robin, now I've swapped that no-hard-shoulder
useless Batmobile for this old Humber;
a real classic with a shiny bumper.
Robin, you're no longer in the picture:
in this hero game it's nags for courses,
now Rodney from Only Fools and Horses
has signed up to be my future partner;
he's taller, harder, stronger, brighter
and that daft suit you wore fits him tighter;
you're history now, a real Boy Blunder.

AT THE TOMB OF THE UNKNOWN ACCOUNTANT

Meet me tonight in the graveyard
when stars climb the graph of the sky,
when Orion skims over horizons
and the moon is a silver coin.

We'll kneel at the double-entry
to the tomb where the great man lies,
clutching the FTSE 100
in the fist of his cheque-signing hand.

With dewy librarian eyes, my dear,
we'll read his great works out aloud:
his Hang Seng Opus, his Dow Jones Dirge,
his Ode to the Banks of the Nile.

At the tomb of the Unknown Accountant
wordsmiths wonder and awe,
who can't rub two pennies together,
whose book-keeping keeps them all poor.

Praise to the numerate masses
of this number-worshipping world.
Praise to their dexterous digits,
their Lottery Roll-Over souls.

Let us invoke all the Mammonite codes.
Let us recite the Lloyds prayer.
Kneel with me here, for we are the meek
and we will inherit fuck all.

PERILS OF THE '60s

(i)

I fell into an avalanche
It covered up my soul
When I'm not this hunchback that you see
I sleep beneath the golden hill

— Leonard Cohen loses his keys in the snow again

(ii)

Sugar, ah, Honey Honey
You are my candy girl
And you got me wanting you

— Bob Dylan runs out of dope while writing
Sad Eyed Lady of the Lowlands

(iii)

Little boxes, little boxes,
Little boxes made of ticky-tacky

— Pete Seeger foresees Thatcher's plan for the homeless

(iv)

Hey baby won't you take a chance—
Put your hands down my underpants.
Let's dance…

—Lyrics discarded by Chris Montez

46

(v)

I remember… Who?

—Tragically, Frank Ifield contracts Alzheimer's mid-song

(vi)

And so it was that later…
Michael Jackson was in jail.
And at first his face just ghostly
Turned a Whiter Shade of Pale

(vii)

Do You Wanna Dance?
I Got you Babe
You've Lost That Loving Feeling
Where Did Our Love go?

— All the lyrics you'll ever need

(viii)

For I'm not made of wood
And I don't have a Wooden Heart

— Pinocchio in denial

PERIDIOTIC TABLE

Element	Properties
Hydrogin	Drunkenness
Hellium	Damnation
Boreon	Tedium
Nightrogen	Darkness
Fagnesium	Coughing
Paluminium	Friendliness
Sillycon	Ridiculousness
Prospherous	Richness
Potatsium	Mashiness
Scandalum	Outrageousness
Titanicum	Disastrousness
Vainadium	Conceit
Mangonese	Fruityness
Zinc	See 'Titanicum'
Arsenic	Bottom Pinching
Bromine	Brotherliness
Krapton	Uselessness
Stropium	Aw-kwardness
Yttrium	Welshness
Idiodine	Stupidity
Xenon	Buddhixm
Noddymium	Childishness
Disturbium	Interruption
Er..bium	Hesitation
Ytterbugium	Jiving
Osmondium	Donnyness
Aridium	Dryness
Bismuth	Mind your own
Plutonium	Cartoonish
Francium	Goes to Hollywoodium

KENNETH'S FATHER'S CANINE IS DECEASED

Ken Dodd's Dad's Dog's Dead.

Dodd's
Dog's
Dead,
Ken.
—Dad.

Dad
Dodd's
Dog's
Dead.
—Ken

Dog's
Dead.
—Ken
Dodd's
Dad.

Dead— Ken Dodd's Dad's Dog.

THUS SPRACH ZEBEDEE

Time for bed!
It's sixty past ten.
Switch off your head,
start snoring again.
Wind up the cat.
Kick out the clock.
Climb into your pit
through the hole in your sock.
First set the telly to TV-a.m.
Draw the curtains in pencil or pen.
Shoot out the lights.
Switch on the dark.
Muzzle the kids
so they don't bark.
Tell them that fairies
give them three wishes.

You have the sex.
I'll do the dishes.

COUNTDOWN

You were five, twelve years ago.
I held your hand up all the stairs,
counting every step to sleep.

I read you rhymes and Fairy Tales,
told you lies about the dark,
counting every step to sleep.

For every Prince a thousand toads,
for every smile a thousand tears,
counting every step to sleep.

I turned around and went back down,
counting my remaining years,
counting every step to sleep.

THE TALISMAN

It was rumoured weeks before...

There were hand signals
across the breakfast table.

They spoke in tongues
on the far side of his newspaper.

On occasions they would sniff the air
as wolves will.

They read horoscopes and tarot cards,
threw yarrow sticks and burned incense.

Then one day the taller one said:
Time to get it, the signs are right.

?

Later on, it arrived, parcelled in fog:
ushered past his question-mark eyes
into the haven of a bedroom.

All day long it burned
and blushed beneath a blouse.

And his daughter
took another step towards the door.

HELPLESS

Your daughter's born. She is helpless.
You teach, you nurture, give her toys.
You bandage cuts and mend the breaks.

Years pass. Your child grows up. It takes
the blink of an eye. She meets boys
in pubs and falls in love. Helpless.

She goes on dates and graduates.
You cling to all the hard-won joys.
Your daughter's gone. You are helpless.

ZERO GRAVITY

Sometimes a sound will stop you in your tracks:
an ice cream van, a fairground hum will waltz
you, fevered, back to that time you danced
to famous, now old-fashioned, songs.
Your fingers, stiffer now it seems,
tap the dashboard to a half-remembered tune.

Traffic lights flash their lazy Disco strobe.
Hazy slo-mo memories drift across your eyes.
The handbrake drops, all the cogs engage.
You feel that zero gravity of age:
your life speeding forward
while your mind is in reverse.

CURTAINS

I went to the dentist.
He gave me a toothache
that lasted for days.

I went to the bank
to spend more time
with my money.

The teller told me
that my stash had split,
destination unknown.

My solicitor said
he was glad I dropped in,
and would I sign these papers?

— *A Citation for Repossession.*
— *My Last Will and Testament.*
— *My Death Certificate.*

I phoned my father
for advice.
He did not answer.

All I heard was
my sister sobbing,
curtains drawing.

WHAT THEY SAY ABOUT YOU

They say that you'll be leaving me tonight,
despite the love I gave for you to keep.
I weep for all that I cannot make right.

The flowers that I brought lie in a heap.
I stoop to pick the vase up from the floor,
you gesture with a tired dismissive sweep.

You seem to be more distant than before—
a door to somewhere else now holds your gaze.
I raise my voice to supplicate, implore

for one more chance, a few forgiving days.
You raise your head, we kiss one last goodnight—
the light is dimmed, the nurses walk away.

They say that you'll be leaving me tonight.

THE MAGIC OF POETRY

Thank you for buying this
modest slim volume,
The Magic of Poetry.

I'm glad you persevered
as far as this page. After all,
I can't pull this off by myself.

You don't mind being a poet's
assistant for a short time, do you?

Good, then let us begin...

I'll take the top two corners
of the page while you grab
the bottom really tight.

Now pull with all your might!

Abracadabra!

Do you see what we've done?
Together we've got to the end
of the page without having
to suffer a single line of poetry.

No, please don't applaud.
It's the oldest trick in the book.

Douglas W Gray

APPRECIATION

for Sheila

I am possessed
with the future,
setting in your stare.

Poet-wise in love
with flesh and form,
though malice springs
from regions of the past.

Now I understand:
what disparage meant,
what abandon meant;
what really, truly matters.

Take this hungry heart.
Conscience kills my soul.

SUBJECT MATTER

Who on earth am I to try and write,
sitting in a shed, anglepoise at hand,
an audience of tins and pots and jars?

I rummage through the dustbin
in my head, which covers half the roof—
need a little oomph, but all I hear is

Leonard Cohen songs, humming from a row
of tacks as shadows start to crawl, cards
and bits of paper, Jesused to the wall.

I'm staring at the stars, sky
an inky-blue, darkening the page
with all these images of you.

DOE

I cursed at the state of the car;
the cost came late at night...

Driving the old coast road:
bits of bumper bleed a trail
to life that's shed its load,
a broth of broken hooves.

There was no thinking distance
in her miles per hour of fright;
gracile in daytime, staring goodnight.
Nothing left to do but watch and pray.

Now I'm the type for bitter steel
at suffering or pain, and feel
for Bambi here, a sick cartoon
of froth and bloody fear.

This is where a life will end
and moments live today:
in velvet brown the years
it took for us to pass away.

STRUCK

I talk to my self, physically stable,
drifting away in the woods
— there's words in here
I haven't smelled for years.

I am like a child,
full of wild surprise,
a rogue impulse for
chocolates, flowers, cards.

I would say I'm sick,
it's eating me away,
everything is
other colour scenes—

images in shadow,
light and cloud domains;
I can't help it,
there you go again...

SCENE

Sundays dad is coffin-laid,
a haze of drink on the grass.

Mum and I sit by the fire
thawing this impasse;

pray to God to end the weekend rite.
Boiling through the afternoon

anger burgles fright,
the infancy of vengeance starts to grow—

spitting venom, like a snake,
I will snap and he will break;

on her mouth a perfect pout of O.

MOTHER

A dressing-down,
the polished floor,
words have clustered,
more and more,
lapping at my ears.
I drown as she waves
in the air.

Indomitably, she
draws breath
between each sip of tea,
swimming in a stare.

INDECENT EXPOSURE

The speed required
blurs the frame—
you struck still life,
in anger I snapped.

Perhaps it's the light
that inhibits,
a slow penumbra
tracking your smile.

The eyes,
though focussed,
do not reflect the soul;
negative, a stranger.

UNDERSTANDING

for Linda

You are clear
in a vision
of the past, grace
as we taste common greed.

Unsound words
in this lofty façade,
tongues on a wound
to make love scratched and torn.

Sweet, sweet pain.
And here I am,
bleeding desire
in scimitar eyes.

Beyond the pale
I hope to flower,
knowing honesty
withers in its spore.

Again the self I lose,
conscious that time
is no more
than reasonable truth.

GEOGRAPHY FROM LOVE

Iceland you claim,
hold the look
of a child at this
peculiar isle.

I counter
with Cyprus—
too cold
that climate here.

Softly we collide,
continental drift,
a flesh frontier
for this stain

on the sheet,
smug as swots
making geography
from love.

COBALT ICE

You paint
a leaving smile
when I'm overcome
by lips and, Jesus,
the eyes, some body's there.

I'm screaming
for the death of this affair,
pull aside the veil,
staring into subterfuge,
the awful truth
like nails.

Ask my punctured heart
you never really met,
filling up with agony
and pumping out regret.

FLUX

Always for me
the night
begins its spree,
a waltz to jig
in bedroom master class.

You shake out a duvet of years—
we cannot find each other;
I do not know myself.

Still we cling to bitching
flotsam, jetsam all our fears,
letting rip with fists
of tears and lies.

Now these lines begin
to bleed, trample through
my heart, burgle sleep
while ghost moons flit the cloud.

GEORGIE

more than holds her drink, ventilates
what others think in verbal Waterloos.
Stakes her claim for equal rights
and doesn't give a shite in public.

Necking beers and popping pills,
a social bitch with virtual cock
who'd fuck around the clock. Men
are changed more frequently than knickers.

Life's philosophy— whore in bed
and angel with the knuckle-duster looks,
who cooks by gas and knocks them out
with head. Oh she's all that,

something else, aches
that analgesics just delay.
And what's the use pretending
that she's gay? She's really not

this little chap with womb
and monthly handicap who 'does
just as she please'. Tell you what,
she don't like what she sees.

DONNA

deals in ecstasy, puts my hand
upon her knee, a hinge, she says,
halfway up to heaven.

Throws me an expectant look
to feed an appetite.

The waters of her heart
have broke.

I'll be her baby tonight.

MAKING AMENDS

There are days the world is
barbs and briars, bleeding
hurt at losing lovers.

Though something else
our travelogue of others, chaos
cast and overblown with flesh.

I'm a clone of want and greed
with afterplay on id,
and you will feed the psyche on a kiss.

We gravitate, towards a mutual bliss.

MARY

Like the testing of Solomon implies,
she wants to assert supremacy...

The most vulnerable moments you come,
ruling thought, wearing nothing but style.

Numb at those eyes, scheming and wild—
you love and I hate and you hate and I love,

until beguiled, at more than dampened pillows.
Black and blue I weep for two, straddle

want and bliss, a perfume prize and novel highs
that smell of rotting touch— too much,

this, when love's a desert, full of fleshy tales,
or nailed to one and loath to resurrect.

FREIGHT

She cowers in the kitchen
while he stammers at the latch,
cooking a come-on that's froze.

More than willing, each night had.
Goodness is wrung from her heart.
The petals of her sex concoct a fist.

She ekes out an allowance,
fear in her head rent-free—
the first bruise bringing flowers;

he swore he'd quit the drink!
She kept her vow and besides.
Sick each morning, sentenced,

bread knife pulled to stop,
churning in a swollen stomach
full of his contempt.

VIEW

In the park the leaves are falling tears.
Looking through her cut glass vision,
facing her nadir...

She'd met him sipping cocktails in a club.
After several drinks she thinks to ask
him to her flat— cup of coffee,
video, bit of this and that.

Giggling through the underpass,
to flirting in his car, and that's as far
as she'd have liked to go.

The euphemisms thud, the bruising
and the blood, a hollow howl
like making love to rage.

What part of *no* is hard to comprehend?
Trust versus lust in a city room
where proof just referees— a stiff November
slaps her face, goes on raping trees.

GREEN

Some climbers are self-clinging, attaching themselves to their supports…

The Royal Horticultural Society: Encyclopaedia of Gardening

All I know of Arthur Emslie is—
at horticulture, 1910, he was
what you'd call *the biz*, and lies
entwined with ivy in the kirk.

She took a stem off his stone,
watched it brood in glass,
wishing it would root,
a limb for the foot of the path.

It blanched as if in brine.
I proposed we throw it out
for a lick of her feline tongue—
what he really wants is love.

So she wooed *him* and cooed *him*
with words, a penile tuber grew,
something she caressed.
It stung like nettles!

She petted and potted her dear,
hugging the wall, hogging the floor,
grabbing at anything near
and changing hue like squid.

Then that bell-shaped flower,
an essence of misery
filling the room, a bloom
unfolding foetal.

I made her bed it by the birch.
It hissed and swayed
in the wind; struck its throat
for a slash on the wrist.

Midnights hold a crying child
to Paraquat my dreams, a brat
who's spoiling as he schemes
and feeds from all but milk.

WAITING

An evil air, something smells
to those in sober suits,
distant from these denims,
twelve-bore boots.

Could be halitosis.
My hair— I don't nit-pick
but a blue rinse,
I swear, looks and turns away.

Dear, I'm a family man,
clean of habit, collar
and, this heroin pallor,
quite legit, won't affect
how close you sit
to one you think has crabs.

I'm no trouble, just a face
grown shy of the blade.
Or it's my bloody feet.
No one takes a seat
that's up for grabs.

CORVUS CORONE

The quiet of an evening until they start
a row— riffs of rasps that fall from rotten boughs.

You riot with a verb against my noun,
picking at the definition of their Latin root,
waxing into lyrical and soundly theorise...

                    I tell you that
I hear your mother, now your sister too,
for hostile looks pursued by hooded eyes.

EVE

Marriage, an execution
of self-interest.

A social theory:
woman pays the debt

from which a man
is physically exempt.

As mother she may bear
the actions of his brunt.

SONG

I'm sitting, as the sun goes down
and electrifies the cloud,
at dying day begin to drown,
cry your name aloud.
Moonlight shines
through the pines
and the sky now rains with fact,
to fall on me
like a love decree;
midnight, the heart attacked...